D0532248

Children of the World

Thailand

For their help in the preparation of *Children of the World: Thailand*, the editors gratefully thank Employment and Immigration Canada, Ottawa, Ont.; the US Immigration and Naturalization Service, Washington, DC; the United States Department of State, Bureau of Public Affairs, Office of Public Communication, Washington, DC, for unencumbered use of material in the public domain; and Chutima Onchaiyapum, Milwaukee, WI.

Library of Congress Cataloging-in-Publication Data

Orihara, Kei.
   Thailand/photography by Kei Orihara; edited by David K. Wright & MaryLee Knowlton.
      p. cm. — (Children of the world)
   Bibliography: p.
   Includes index.
   Summary: Presents the life of a girl in northern Thailand discussing her family and the history, political system, and traditions of her country.
   ISBN 1-555-32223-9 (lib. bdg.).
   1. Thailand — Social life and customs — Juvenile literature. 2. Children — Thailand — Juvenile literature. [1. Thailand — Social life and customs. 2. Family life — Thailand.] I. Wright, David K. II. Knowlton, MaryLee. III. Title. IV. Series: Children of the world (Milwaukee, Wis.)
DS568.075 1988
779'.99593—dc19   88-21050

North American edition first published in 1988 by

Gareth Stevens, Inc.
7317 West Green Tree Road
Milwaukee, Wisconsin 53223, USA

Typeset by Zahn-Klicka-Hill, Milwaukee.
Map design: Sheri Gibbs.

1 2 3 4 5 6 7 8 9 93 92 91 90 89 88

Children of the World
Thailand

Photography by
Kei Orihara

Edited by
David K. Wright &
MaryLee Knowlton

Gareth Stevens Publishing
Milwaukee

. . . a note about *Children of the World:*

The children of the world live in fishing towns, Arctic regions, and urban centers, on islands and in mountain valleys, on sheep ranches and fruit farms. This series follows one child in each country through the pattern of his or her life. Candid photographs show the children with their families, at school, at play, and in their communities. The text describes the dreams of the children and, often through their own words, tells how they see themselves and their lives.

Each book also explores events that are unique to the country in which the child lives, including festivals, religious ceremonies, and national holidays. The *Children of the World* series does more than tell about foreign countries. It introduces the children of each country and shows readers what it is like to be a child in that country.

. . . and about *Thailand:*

Eleven-year-old Maana lives in the northern part of Thailand. Thailand is one of the world's major rice-producing nations; and like most Thais, Maana and his family are farmers. But Maana's family raises mostly fruits and vegetables. Their farm was started by Maana's great-grandparents, who paddled up the river to reach their land.

To enhance this book's value in libraries and classrooms, comprehensive reference sections include up-to-date data about Thailand's geography, demographics, currency, education, culture, industry, and natural resources. *Thailand* also features a bibliography, research topics, activity projects, and discussions of such subjects as Bangkok, the country's history, political system, ethnic and religious composition, and language.

The living conditions and experiences of children in Thailand vary tremendously according to economic, environmental, and ethnic circumstances. The reference sections help bring to life for young readers the diversity and richness of the culture and heritage of Thailand. Of particular interest are discussions of the country's fascinating and often precarious relationship to other nations of Southeast Asia, particularly Vietnam, Laos, and Kampuchea (Cambodia).

CONTENTS

Maana and his family. Top row: Somnug, his father; Panyee, his mother; brother Sainaam.
Bottom row: Maana; sister Tuan Jai; and brother Pani.

Maana's house is built of wood and raised on stilts.

LIVING IN THAILAND:
Maana from the Green Earth

Maana Nonghord is an 11-year-old boy from a small village near Sawankhalok, a city in northern Thailand. In this country, more than 70% of the people are farmers, like Maana's family. The land is good for growing. Maana's house is wrapped in greenery all year round.

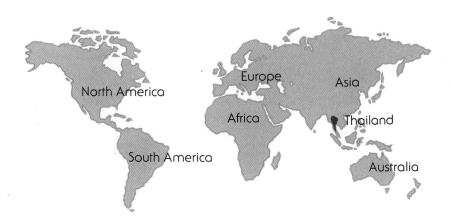

North America

Europe

Asia

Africa

Thailand

South America

Australia

Kingdom of Thailand

Burma

Laos

Sawankhalok

Bangkok

Kampuchea

Vietnam

Life on the River

The Yom River runs past Sawankhalok. On its way to Bangkok, almost 250 miles (400 km) to the south, the Yom becomes part of Thailand's great Chao Phraya River.

Today, Bangkok is a city of at least 7 million people, but when it was still a tiny village, Maana's ancestors paddled up the river together, looking for fertile land of their own. They spent many days on the river. He likes to hear his parents tell stories about his ancestors' battles with tigers and crocodiles on the river banks. Their long journey ended where the land was fertile and food was sure to be plentiful!

In the Thai language, the people call their river *maenam* after the mother of water. They use the river for travel, for drinking, and for irrigating their land. Children and adults alike play in the water and cool themselves during the hot days. The river is the center of their community.

In early evening, the children play in the river.

Three silly boys come home with grapefruits for a snack. Guess where they are!

People take off their shoes and wash their feet before entering a house.

The neighbors' yards are playgrounds for the children.

Maana's Village

Life in the village is peaceful. There are few television sets blaring in homes and hardly any cars on the roads. In a farming community, no one goes hungry. So people enjoy the quiet pace.

The villagers help each other with their chores and share the few things they own.

In the evening, people go visiting. If they arrive during dinner time, the woman of the family will greet visitors by saying "*Gin kao*," which means "have dinner with us." The visitors reply "*Im lao*," which means "I'm full." It is polite to offer food, but if visitors believe there may not be quite enough food in the home for the whole family, they will pretend to be full.

The children are as generous as their parents. Even at school, they share food with classmates. Maana and Pani carry a lunch box with food for themselves and a dish to share.

Maana and Pani leave for school with their lunch box.

Maana races to the landing dock for the river ferry.

School on the River

The children from the village go to school across the river. The Wat Saiyio Elementary School is just up the embankment from the boat landing. It has 107 students from first grade to sixth grade. Maana's fifth grade class has 19 students.

Like most schools in the countryside, Wat Saiyio Elementary School is next to a Buddhist *wat*, or temple.

Most Thais are Buddhist, and their schools are part of their temples. Every morning, the children clasp their hands and give thanks to Buddha and to their country, which upholds the Buddhist faith.

The children take the ferry to school.

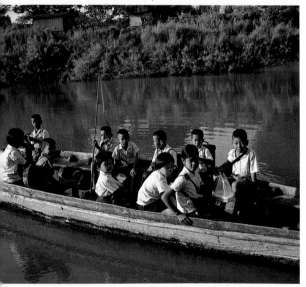

They climb the embankment to reach the school.

The students and teachers start their day with prayers at morning assembly.

Maana is studying math, Thai, science, social studies, religion and culture, music, dance, and physical education. He also has classes in manual crafts and home skills. In these classes the children learn cooking, sewing, carpentry, and bicycle and tool repair.

All public school students in Thailand study English. In Bangkok, students start learning how to read and write English in first grade. In more rural areas, students begin English classes in fifth grade.

As he grew up, Maana learned some English from his older brother and sister, so he is quite confident, and English is his favorite class.

13

The children gather to have their picture taken. They are a cheerful bunch!

Today the teacher says, "You've studied hard enough today. Let's take turns performing something for the class." The children are thrilled. For the next hour, they get up in front of the class and do something they are good at: dancing, singing, comic routines, and mimicry. They all perform well and the room is filled with clapping, cheering, and laughter.

The sixth grade classroom is in another building.
Many Thai buildings are built with open construction.

Performance time!

Drinking ladles made from coconuts.

His pack holds all Maana needs for school.

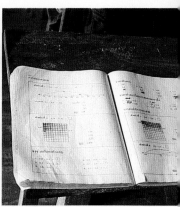

A math textbook.

The children sit in a circle around the food they have brought for lunch.

After lunch they always brush their teeth.

It's lunch time. The students sit in a circle in the hallway. They put the food they've brought to share in the middle. Anyone can take food from any of the containers, so everyone has a variety of foods.

Physical education class always starts with two laps around the field.

Get off to a good start!

Maana loves physical education class. Class begins with two laps around the field and warm-up exercises. The students know the routine and do their laps and warm-ups without supervision. Today, for the first time, they practice how to get a good start for a footrace. The teacher shows them how to get started without falling on their faces.

Table tennis with a board, not a net.

Crocheting during recess.

Mak ruk is like chess. The board and pieces are made from scraps of cloth, paper, and old bottle caps.

The whole school plays a game of Thai tag.

Most of the students at Wat Saiyio Elementary School come from farming families. Only about half of them will continue in school after sixth grade. Maana doesn't like studying and wants to be a farmer, so he doesn't plan to go on to school. His little brother Pani loves studying and wants to go as far as he can. Their parents want them to do whatever will satisfy them.

Volleyball is fun in the grass and dirt.

The path home from the boat landing, green and quiet.

Buddhist monks are everywhere.

A Buddhist Boy

Every morning, just before seven, Maana and Pani go out to the path in front of their home carrying food. They are waiting for the monks who come wearing yellow robes and carrying bowls.

Maana and his friends spoon the rice and other food into the metal bowls. Then the monks chant a short prayer for them. "May this food which you have offered return to you and give you bountiful hearts." Maana and the others crouch on the ground and pray.

Thailand is a Buddhist country. The Thai people take care of their monks. The villagers know that the monks serve Buddha for the benefit of all. So they help the monks any way they can.

What game is this?

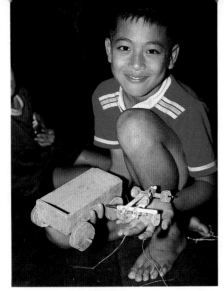

A homemade truck.

Rhinoceros beetles — big but harmless.

Maana is a clown, no doubt about it.

In Thailand most boys and men go into a *wat* at least once to lead a monk's life. Some go for a month, just before they marry. Others go when a relative dies so that their prayers will hasten the relative's journey to heaven. Or they can spend as little as a day in a wat. The first time Maana went was when he was six years old. He has gone three times since then, staying a day each time.

Buddhists believe that rivers, trees, and even rice grains have spirits or goddesses that protect them. The goddess of rice is Mae Phra Prasop. Nang Tani is the female spirit who protects the banana trees. From Indian culture come goddesses of the earth and its rivers. Many Thai girls are named after these goddesses.

23

One of the ten water urns.

Cleaning the floor.

Folding the bedding.

The butcher is Maana's uncle.

Maana at Work

Work is a part of Maana's day, too. All the village children help their families. Each morning Maana and Pani wash the dishes from dinner the night before. Their sister, Tuan Jai, draws water from the village well. She hangs buckets from a pole balanced on her shoulders and fills the household's ten water urns. She must make five trips up and down the stairs.

Maana can get his work done and still have time to play because his village does not have as many forms of entertainment as cities do. Some people have radios, but there are only a couple of television sets.

About 90% of all the cars and trucks in Thailand are in Bangkok, so Maana doesn't travel to find things to do. He stays busy in his home and village.

Picking fruit takes teamwork.

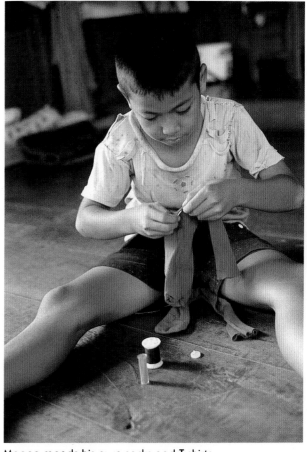

Maana mends his own socks and T-shirts.

Digging for clams in the river.

Picking *pakchee*, parsley, for dinner.

Maana at Play

From the time they return from school until dinner, the yard and the village are a playground for Maana and Pani and all the village children.

The village has no toy store, so people make most of their own toys. One of Maana's treasures is a slingshot that his father made for him when he was just three. Children learn to make their own fishing poles and hooks by watching their parents. They don't buy materials for what they make. Instead they save whatever they can. Before they throw away lumber scraps or old rubber thongs, they think about what they can make from them.

Playing with fireworks.

Maana's treasures.

A musical instrument made from bottle caps and wire.

27

Thai foods have many different flavors.

Maana's parents cook dinner together.

Fish caught by Poo and pakchee picked by Maana and Pani.

An Evening in Thailand — Food and Friends

Mae and Poo, mother and father, cook dinner together every night. Poo catches the fish and shellfish in the river. Mae and the children collect the vegetables, fruits, and spices from the garden and neighborhood. Nothing is from packages. The food is spicy and hot, which stimulates the appetite.

An oven for charcoal cooking.

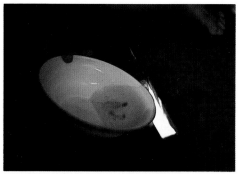

Throwing dirty dishwater under the house for the dogs and chickens.

Pans of water keep ants from climbing up the legs.

The family eats rice from bowls. They hold the rice in their fingers and dip it in the sauces. More recently, they sometimes use spoons.

Maana makes great omelettes. He mixes black pepper with eggs and fries them. He then eats them dipped in *nam prik*, a hot sauce made from red pepper, garlic, and a fish-based sauce. Nam prik is a part of every meal.

Med manglak, or dried seeds.

Manako, or papaya.

Kanung, or jackfruit.

Kanumkaok, or baked rice cakes.

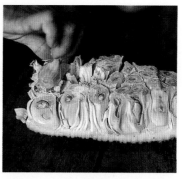

The villagers learn about the outside world from television. Owning a television is rare in Thailand.

The next-door neighbors entertain their friends with a concert.

Visiting Time

In the evening the villagers go visiting. Maana's family recently bought a television, so their house is a popular gathering place. Poo's rule is: No TV except on Saturday and Sunday. But when their neighbors arrive, he smiles and turns it on.

After a little TV, the whole group goes next door. The neighbors have prepared a concert for their friends. They all play instruments: the *kantyai,* a drum; the *ranad,* like a xylophone; and the *randlek,* which is a glockenspiel.

The rhythm is so festive and inviting that the children begin dancing. The performers are all farmers, but they have learned from professionals and are wonderful to listen to. This is how the villagers entertain themselves. They don't need to go to the city and spend money to enjoy themselves.

Doing homework with friends seems to be more fun.

Making rice cakes from sticky rice and coconut milk.

Pani makes a lantern for *Loi Krathong,* the lantern-floating festival, coming in November.

A Village Wedding

A wedding in Sawankhalok brings joy. Early in the morning, the voices of monks chanting *sutras*, or Buddhist teachings, resound throughout the village. On mats with flowered patterns the bride, bridegroom, and their guests sit facing the monks. For two hours the sutras ring out.

The bride and groom are childhood friends.

Guests wish luck to the bride and groom.

White thread is used as a charm to prevent misfortune. For the wedding, the heads of the bride and groom are wound with thread and the ends are tied to the monk who performs the marriage ceremony. When the chanting is over, the two unwind the thread from their heads, kneel before the guests, and present their wrists to be bound together. This thread represents their lifetime bond. Then the entertainment begins. The villagers eat, drink, and laugh until after sunset.

Offerings from next door.

The men and boys make a lot of noise.

Sweet foods for the guests.

A sideshow with its own "groom."

Rice turns golden as it ripens.

Mae at the Morning Market

Mae gets up at 4 o'clock on market mornings. The bus leaves at 5 o'clock for the market in the city of Sawankhalok. It's not yet light when she leaves the house, groping in the dark for the path to the bus stop.

She walks through the market with a pole over her shoulders. On the ends of the pole are two wicker baskets bulging with bananas. These baskets are too heavy to carry by hand.

Hauling produce down from the bus roof.

Mae's first customer. It's still dark.

Everything is sold by 10 o'clock, so Mae goes shopping.

Orchids are sold in bunches.

Women run the market.

The money Mae makes at the market is the only cash income the family has until harvest season. So Mae goes to the market every three days to sell fruits and vegetables and banana leaves, which are used as wrappings.

She buys some treats for Maana and Pani. They like the packets of watermelon and candy sold by a vendor at the market.

While she is in Sawankhalok, Mae shops for her family. She buys school supplies and clothing with some of the money she makes by selling fruits and vegetables. Most villages have no phones, so sometimes women at the market will use the city's public phones. Mae has never made a phone call in her life — no one she knows has a phone and she has had little contact with anyone outside the village who might have one.

Deep-fried soybean curd snacks.

Sweet-sour makaam and watermelon.

Lunches prepared and wrapped.

Thai candy and treats.

Many Thai women work outside the home — on farms or in factories. In the country, fewer women work outside the home. Women do most of the buying and selling at the markets. Educated women work as teachers, nurses, government workers, and businesspeople. But men still run most of the political matters in Thailand.

The women of the marketplace are close. They trade stories about their families and lend money to each other. Most of them do not see each other except at the market, so they look forward to market day!

Mae walks back to the bus stop.

Cutting down bananas.

Picking makaam.

A good day's catch.

Working in the soybean field.

Mae and Poo meet under the makaam tree.

Working the Land and the River

The family's farmland is so vast that even Maana's father does not know how much land there is. The family harvests fruit between April and May, and soybeans and corn during June. They plant banana, mango, coconut, papaya, and jackfruit trees together, in the same orchard.

Drenched with sweat, Poo and Mae work for hours under the sun. After working hard, it is a relief to go fishing. The neighbors share the nets that they stretch across the river. During the rainy season the nets are always full.

The ruins of the great kingdom of Sukhothai.

Villagers in a funeral procession. The children in yellow are boy monks.

South of Maana's village is the city of Sukhothai, where the ancestors of today's Thais first unified their nation about 750 years ago. But the Thai people have been in the country for over 5,000 years. They migrated from southwest China, seeking fertile land where they could plant their rice paddies.

In this area of rice paddies and forests are remains of old temples with large statues of Buddha. The Thais still value these ancient sites.

A lantern float moves through Sukhothai Historical Park.

A fire-breathing snake made of petals.

Lanterns in the shape of lotus flowers.

Artwork made of black peppers, beans, and rice.

Loi Krathong Festival

The Loi Krathong, or lantern-floating, is Thailand's oldest festival. The people give thanks to the spirit of rivers. On the day of the full moon at the end of the rainy season, farmers float lanterns, or *krathong*, made of banana leaves on the river.

Maana has taken part in this great festival every year near the village. But this year's festival is special. His father is taking him to the Loi Krathong in Sukhothai.

The festival starts in the morning with a parade of people dressed in Thai costumes. Festival music, water buffaloes, and elephants are part of the celebration. Schoolchildren make lanterns from leaves or flower petals and carry them in the parade.

A parade of elephants.

Maana and Pani buy snacks at a roadside stand.

Fire and light tell the story of the dawn of the proud Sukhothai Dynasty, the beginning of the Thai nation.

People gather around the pond to watch the floating lanterns.

The climax of the festival is the great drama of light. When the ruins are lit by fireworks against the dark sky, it feels like the flash of battle fire. Maana's eyes widen. His heart beats rapidly. Before long, quiet returns, and people release balloons lit by flames into the night sky. A dance begins to the rhythm of drums. On the water, the lanterns glitter a bright red and yellow.

This national festival recalls a time before Buddhism. It was a time when people all over the world believed that everything had spirits — water, trees, animals, rivers, people, and the earth itself. People feared and respected these spirits, much as the Thais still do today. Rivers, for example, are considered to be more powerful than humans, and their spirits are eternal.

Maana imagines that he is piling bad feelings left over from fights and sicknesses onto his lantern. Then he releases the lantern with its imaginary load onto the maenam — along with a prayer that the spirit of the river will renew his spirit.

A lantern burns brightly.

The children and their father gaze at the water.

FOR YOUR INFORMATION:
Thailand

Official Name: Prathet Thai
(pruh-TAH TIE)
Kingdom of Thailand

Capital: Bangkok

History

Early History

The people we think of as Thais first lived in southwest China. They grew rice in flooded fields, or paddies. When they found that the area around the Chao Phraya river, in present-day Thailand, was ideal for rice paddies, they began to move there. There is evidence that people have lived there for over 5,000 years.

A statue of Gautama, the father of Buddhism.

By 1238, the Thais had founded the kingdom of Sukhothai, which means "dawn of happiness." They consider this the beginning of the Thai nation. In 1350, a ruler named Rama Tibodi overpowered his rivals and founded the kingdom of Ayutthaya. His rich, powerful kingdom became a major center of trade.

Thailand was called Siam when the first Europeans visited the country in 1511. Siam was a powerful nation that was protected somewhat from invasions by other nations because it was not on a major sailing route between India and China. These two countries had goods that began to interest other nations.

But Thailand's geographical position did not protect it from quarrels with its neighbors. For nearly 400 years the Ayutthaya kingdom prospered, but it fought Cambodians and Burmese on its borders. For many centuries, however, the Thai people controlled the country.

In 1767, the Burmese invaded and destroyed the city of Ayutthaya. They made their capital at the city of Thon Buri, near the present capital of Bangkok. In 1782, after another uprising, Thailand's present line of kings came to power. The first king, Pya Chakri, took the name Rama I. He moved the capital to Bangkok.

Western Influences

After 1800, the Thais saw the British take over Burma and Malaysia. The French conquered and colonized Vietnam, Laos, and Cambodia. Siam was surrounded by these colonies and China was just to its north. To avoid being swallowed up by these more powerful nations, the Thais decided they would have to develop, to become more modern.

King Mongkut, who ruled from 1851 to 1868, had studied Western history and ideas. He invited Westerners into Siam to help him modernize his country's schools, trading policies, and government. His son, King Chulalongkorn, who ruled from 1868 to 1910, got rid of slavery and other practices from ancient times. He made sure his army had modern weapons and saw to it that the government operated efficiently. He often visited Europe, bringing back ideas he liked. For instance, he brought railroads, the telegraph, and a public school system.

Western Conquests in Southeast Asia

The French and British thought they knew what was best for the Thais. So they decided to watch over the kingdom. But they never entered Siam as conquerors, so today, the people feel like equals to Europeans. They are proud of their native traditions. That is not true of all nations in Southeast

Asia. In fact, this country is still the only one in Southeast Asia that was never taken over by a European country.

Siam becomes Thailand

In many ways, Siam was becoming a modern country. But as the world entered the 20th century, the king still had all of the power.

Many of Siam's military and government leaders knew about other forms of government from their contact with Europe. When it came to forms of government, some began to think that their own country should be more like European countries. In 1932, a group of them forced the king to give up some of his powers.

The king left the throne in 1935, turning it over to his 10-year-old nephew. Civilian leaders wanted to reform the government, but the army pushed them aside. In 1939, Siam officially changed its name to Thailand, which means "land of the free."

World War II and After

In 1941, Japan invaded Thailand, and when Japan attacked Pearl Harbor in 1941, Thailand's government sided with Japan. The government signed a treaty with the Japanese in 1942, and declared war against the United States and Britain that same year.

But as the war turned against Japan, many Thais joined groups allied with Britain and the United States. Thailand came away from the war unharmed — except for giving up rice demanded by Britain and a bit of territory the Japanese had promised to give them. In 1946, the country was admitted to the United Nations.

When the king was found shot to death under mysterious circumstances that same year, the army took control. Then different groups within the army took turns fighting for control of the country. After communist forces took over China in 1949, the Thai government feared a possible invasion by the Chinese. The United States government began offering Thailand military aid in the early 1950s. The Thais allied themselves with the United States. In 1954, Thailand joined the Southeast Asia Treaty Organization. This group was designed to protect the countries of that area against communist invasion.

But the people of Thailand were divided. In the north and east, some people supported the communists. In other areas, people remained neutral. Neutralists didn't want to be close friends with either communist or democratic countries. But eventually Thailand's military leaders allowed the United States to build air bases in Thailand. The American military used these bases heavily during the Vietnam War. Later, the Thais themselves sent troops to fight in Vietnam.

Rural Communism—and Refugees

China supported communists in the Thai countryside. Thai communists became more active as the Thai army fought the Viet Cong and North Vietnamese. After American troops left Southeast Asia in 1973, student demonstrators led a movement that caused the Thai government to fall. The new civilian government became more neutral and, in time, wrote a new constitution.

Several governments quickly followed. One of them requested that US planes and soldiers leave Thailand by 1976. The Thai army did not like the idea of losing American support and began a violent political campaign against the government and its supporters. Numerous governments supported by the military have come and gone since then. In the last few years, supporters of communist goals appear to have lost some of their influence among people living in rural areas.

Throughout the 19th and 20th centuries, the Thai people have admired the king and the royal family. While they have modernized their country, they retain a historic love for their king, and he is concerned about the common people. The current king, Bhumibol Adulyadej, can often be seen in rural areas, asking questions and helping solve problems.

In recent years, refugees have created problems and challenges for Thailand, its government, and its people. Nearly half a million people from Kampuchea, Laos, and Vietnam are in Thai refugee camps, waiting for a chance to live in a free country. The Thais are not rich, but they have been very generous to these people. Thai soldiers protect the refugees from Communist soldiers. Other Thais see to it that the refugees receive food and clothing. Little by little, refugees are resettling in other countries. Thailand, its royal family, and its people have been praised by many international organizations for helping the refugees.

Government

Bhumibol Adulyadej, the current king of Thailand, was born in 1927. He became king in 1946 after his brother, King Ananda Mahidol, died of a gunshot wound. The king is married to Queen Sirikit and has a son, Maha Vajiralongkorn, the crown prince. While Thais love and respect the royal family, the king is not particularly powerful.

Today, the prime minister runs the country. When a coup, the overthrow of the government, takes place, the disagreement is usually between generals who want civilians in the government and generals who do not. Military leaders still hold a great deal of power in Thailand's government.

There is an elected National Assembly, but sometimes some of its representatives are put in office by the government. Political parties are legal, but a trend away from parties seems to be emerging. Instead, people group together according to their work or their social or economic class. Farmers, for example, are joining together to criticize the economic and social policies of the government when these policies do not solve the problems of farmers.

Cities elect their own mayors and councils. Rural villagers choose someone from their village. By tradition, the national government's power ends at the village gate. In other words, Thais are in control of their own local matters.

Currency

The Thai unit of currency is the *baht*. About 21 baht equal one US dollar.

Population and Ethnic Groups

About 53 million people live in Thailand. Nearly 75% of them are Thai and 14% are Chinese, but minority groups, particularly refugees, are growing.

Over 10% of Thailand's people live in Bangkok alone. But most Thais—about 80% of them—live in rural areas. Typical Thais farm and live in a village surrounded by rice paddies. They might have radios, but probably do not have television sets or cars. Only about 10% of the cars and trucks in Thailand can be found outside Bangkok!

Thailand has a large number of hill tribes that are among the world's most interesting people. These primitive tribes look quite different from the Thais and from each other. Some of them move from one place to another after one or two agricultural seasons.

These tribes—including the Hmong, Karen, Lawa, Meo, and Yao—are under pressure from several directions today, partly because of their "slash-and-burn" agricultural practices. This means they cut down or burn parts of the jungle, plant crops, and then move on when the land is no longer fertile. They live in an area called the Golden Triangle, a place near China where Burma, Thailand, and Laos come together. They live simply, which delights tourists who come to observe and learn about them.

But some tribal members also grow opium poppies, which concerns Western governments. These poppies wind up as heroin on European and American streets. Thailand has encouraged these people to grow other things besides opium poppies and has severe penalties for anyone caught selling or using narcotics. But the laws have not always been enforced, and nothing tribal members grow pays as well as the illegal flowers.

The tribes also feel pressure from governments in the area. They like the freedom of moving about whenever they wish to farm new areas, but some countries do not like tribal members moving back and forth without passports or permission.

There are a few other minorities in the country. Persons of Chinese descent are common in most cities. Far to the south, along the Malay Peninsula, there are groups of Malay Muslims, followers of the religion of Islam. Their appearance and language set them apart from the Thais. These people sometimes urge that southern Thailand become part of neighboring Malaysia, where Islam is the official religion.

Women in traditional costumes during Loi Krathong Festival.

Climate

Thailand is usually hot. Sometimes it's hot and dry, as in March through May. Sometimes it's hot and rainy, as in June through October. Between November and February, cooler winds drift south from China. But "cool" in Thailand in the middle of winter can average 62° F (17° C)! The average year-round temperature is between 75° and 86° F (24° to 30° C).

People seeking relief from the heat go to the mountainous north, where there are occasional frosts. Sea breezes bring relief to the southern coast. In some parts of the country, cool, dry winter air produces fogs that last each day until about noon. Annual rainfall amounts vary from about 220 inches (559 cm) in the west to less than 60 inches (152 cm) in the area ranging from the Chao Phraya basin, where Bangkok is, to the northeastern plateaus.

THAILAND — Political and Physical

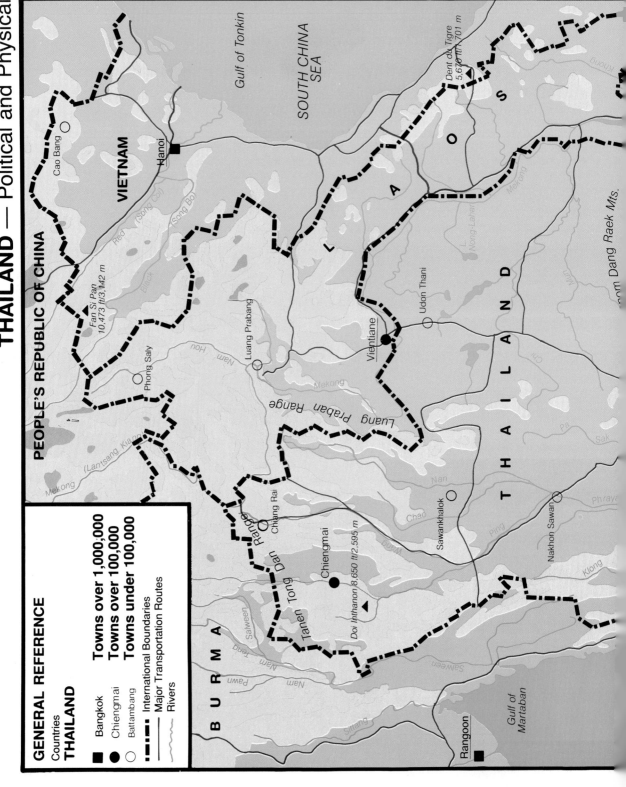

PEOPLE'S REPUBLIC OF CHINA

GENERAL REFERENCE

Countries
THAILAND

■ Bangkok	**Towns over 1,000,000**
● Chiengmai	**Towns over 100,000**
○ Battambang	**Towns under 100,000**
▬▪▬	International Boundaries
──	Major Transportation Routes
～	Rivers

VIETNAM

Cao Bang

Hanoi

Red (Song Coi)

Song Bo

Fan Si Pan
10,473 ft/3,142 m

Black

Phong Saly

Nam Hou

Luang Prabang

Mekong (Lan'tsang Kiang)

Mekong

Luang Praban Range

LAOS

Gulf of Tonkin

SOUTH CHINA SEA

Dent du Tigre
5,670 ft/1,701 m

Kong

Nong Lahan

Udon Thani

Vientiane

Mekong

THAILAND

Nan

Sak

Pa

Chao

Phraya

Nam Hou

Dom Dang Raek Mts.

BURMA

Tanen Tong Dan Range

Salween

Nam Teng

Pawn

Nam Tam

Sittang

Chiang Rai

Chiengmai

Doi Inthanon 8,650 ft/2,595 m

Sawankhalok

Yom

Ping

Wang

Nakhon Sawan

Klong

Salween

Gulf of Martaban

Rangoon

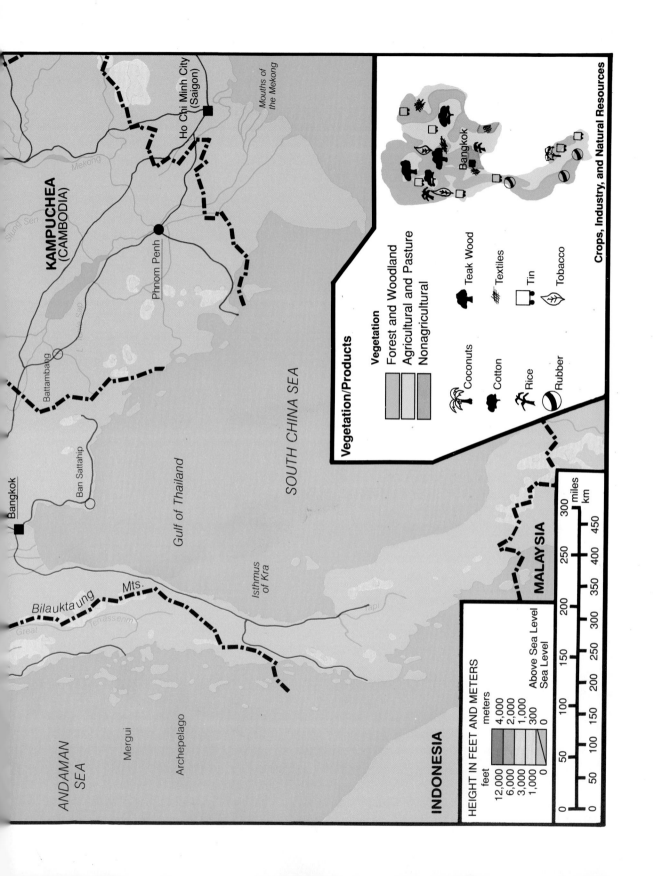

Crops, Industry, and Natural Resources

KAMPUCHEA
(CAMBODIA)

Mekong

Stung Sen

L. Tonle Sap

Phnom Penh

Battambang

Ho Chi Minh City
(Saigon)

Mouths of
the Mekong

SOUTH CHINA SEA

Gulf of Thailand

Ban Sattahip

Bangkok

ANDAMAN
SEA

Mergui

Archepelago

Bilauktaung Mts.

Tenasserim

Great

Isthmus
of Kra

Tapi

MALAYSIA

INDONESIA

Bangkok

Vegetation/Products

Vegetation
Forest and Woodland
Agricultural and Pasture
Nonagricultural

Coconuts
Cotton
Rice
Rubber

Teak Wood
Textiles
Tin
Tobacco

HEIGHT IN FEET AND METERS

feet   meters
12,000 4,000
6,000   2,000
3,000   1,000
1,000   300
0   0   Above Sea Level
            Sea Level

0   50   100 150 200 250 300 miles
0 50 100 150 200 250 300 350 400 450 km

Land

Thailand is 198,456 square miles (514,135 sq km). It is almost as large as the Canadian provinces of Newfoundland and New Brunswick together, or the states of Utah and Colorado combined. Thailand's neighbors include Burma to the west and northwest, Laos on the northeast, Kampuchea to the southeast, and Malaysia to the south. The Gulf of Thailand forms most of the country's southern border. The Andaman Sea forms a small part of the western border.

Mountains lie in the north and along the western border. Their long, tree-covered ridges rise as high as 8,514 feet (2,595 m) above sea level. Over the centuries, ground water has carved caves in limestone hills. Low, rolling hills form most of the northeast and eastern borders. Part of Thailand's border with Laos includes the mighty Mekong River.

The Chao Phraya (Maenam) River.

The area around the Mekong is swampy. To the west, the central plains form a vast fertile area called the Chao Phraya basin. Annual flooding of the Chao Phraya River renews the soil in the area.

Finally, there are some mountains to the southeast, near and along the border with Kampuchea. The peninsula, in short, has hardly any flat land.

Natural Resources

Tin is Thailand's leading mineral export. In fact, Thailand is one of the world's major tin producers, with about an eighth of the world's tin. About 650 mines can be found in southern and southwestern Thailand. Other important mining and quarrying operations produce coal, iron ore, gypsum, manganese, lead, zinc, tungsten, limestone, marble, and gold.

More than half of the country is covered with forests. Thailand's rich forests have many kinds of trees not found in more temperate areas of the world. These trees make the country an excellent place for producing not only paper and plywood, but rubber, rattan, and bamboo. But its main forest product is a rich, dark wood called teak. Villagers use elephants to help harvest teak and other fine hardwoods.

Not everything of value has to be mined or grown. In northern Thailand's Nan Valley, there's a town called Phrae. Here, near the Yom River, people have dug out gemstones with their hands. Local residents and natives travel all over this area, digging, listening to rumors of big finds, and hoping that they might soon be rich. Commonly found stones include sapphires in a variety of colors. In recent years, Thailand, in fact, has become the world's best source of sapphires and rubies!

Several rivers have dams with generators that make electricity. While Thailand does have its own deposits of oil and natural gas, it gets most of its energy from imported oil and coal-fired electric power plants.

Agriculture and Industry

Only about 10% of Thailand's workers work in manufacturing jobs. About three of every four Thais are farmers. Their ability and the country's good growing conditions have made Thailand the world's leading exporter of rice. Two or more crops of paddy rice a year are harvested throughout the central part of the country. Tribespeople grow rice in the hills, too, where they eat what is called dry rice. Unlike the kind grown in paddies, it is a glutinous, or sticky, rice.

Other sizable crops include sugar cane, corn, and palm trees, grown for their edible oil. Thais harvest fruits and vegetables for domestic and foreign markets. They are able to grow enough cotton to create attractive cloth goods for themselves and international markets. The cotton goods are popular with buyers from foreign nations who come to Thailand to purchase materials to market in their own countries.

Living Off the Land

It takes a lot of time and effort to grow a family's food. In a developed country, people just go to a supermarket, shop quickly, and then store food in cans and packages, often in their refrigerator or freezer. But Thais and other people in less-developed countries have to get their food every day because they have few reliable ways to preserve food from bacteria, bugs, rats, and other hungry insects and animals. While the food is fresh, it must be eaten quickly.

But the Thais are fortunate. Farmers grow much more rice than people can eat. Money from selling surplus rice to other countries helps farmers buy items such as salt, clothing, and other manufactured goods. As Thailand becomes more industrialized, fewer people will farm and more will work in factories. Food processing—canning and bottling food grown in Thailand—is already a major industry, serving Thais and foreign markets.

Languages

Thai is the official language. It is spoken by about 90% of the people. Originally, Thai was similar to Chinese, but later it was influenced by Cambodian and Indian languages. It has its own alphabet, one that might look strange to anyone who reads only English, which uses the Roman alphabet.

Thai is hard to speak because it is a tonal language. This means that a one-syllable word such as "my" can have several different meanings, depending on how high or low a tone the speaker uses. In southeastern Thailand, there may be as many as eight different tones for one word.

There are four main Thai dialects, but a standard Thai is taught in school. Hill tribes in the north and east speak their own languages. Persons of Chinese descent, who frequently live in Bangkok, speak Chinese, and Malay is common among Thais who live far to the south. English, too, is taught in many schools.

Education

After kindergarten, children must complete at least six years of school. Thailand's public elementary schools are free, but private elementary schools charge tuition. Elementary schools attached to *wats*, Buddhist temples, are also free. Most high schools are private and charge tuition. There are not enough schools to educate all Thai children as the government and people would like. In Thailand's public grade schools, there are about 31 students for every teacher. Only about one child out of ten graduates from high school.

Boys have better opportunities than girls to attend college. That is because boys can live in a Buddhist temple while going to classes, but girls cannot. The literacy rate is high—about 85% of all Thais can read and write.

Religion

About 95% of all Thais are Buddhists. In fact, Buddhism, which began in India, is the main religion of most of Southeast Asia and China. Buddhism started about the same time the Thais were first venturing into Thailand, about 500 BC. A prince named Gautama believed he could reach nirvana, or heaven, by thinking and acting properly. He did not seem interested in a religion involving a god or gods.

Buddha, as Gautama came to be known, taught his religious and ethical ideas to numerous monks. They then founded monasteries and taught

Buddha's message to others. The religion spread to Thailand, where it is practiced today as colorfully and completely as anywhere on Earth.

Many Thai boys spend at least three months living in a temple, studying Buddhism. They look just like monks, with shaved heads and saffron, or orange yellow, robes. The monks and these boys often beg for money to support themselves. Buddhism allows women to be believers, but they cannot be monks or deal with or touch a monk.

Small numbers of Muslims, Christians, and Confucianists live throughout Thailand. Many members of the hill tribes are animists, or people who believe that all things, including animals, trees, and even rocks, have souls.

Arts and Crafts

Visitors come away from Thailand with jewelry made of gold, jade, opals, sapphires, or rubies. But the real art of Thailand can be found in the many temples and images devoted to Buddha. Thai religious architecture is usually decorated with gold and is always magnificent.

There are other arts and crafts. Hill tribes produce woven cloth that is prized for its complex designs. Thai silk is in demand worldwide. Porcelain and pottery making, skills handed down long ago from China, show country or religious scenes. So do paintings, often found on temple walls. Thai music has been influenced by the Chinese, while the dancers who accompany the music perform ancient dances that came from India or Sri Lanka.

Sports and Recreation

The Thais enjoy a wide range of sports. The most popular team sport is soccer. Children and adults alike play it, and the top teams are followed closely through radio, television, and newspapers. Badminton, tennis, table tennis, volleyball, track and field, swimming, and bicycle racing also have large followings.

Men practice a martial art known as kick boxing. It is just what the name says—hitting with boxing gloves and kicking with bare feet. Kick boxing is only for adults. But everyone enjoys playing *takro,* a game using a wicker ball. Players form a circle and try to keep the ball in the air—without using hands. It helps to know how to play soccer when playing takro!

Sometimes it's too hot to play an active sport. So the Thais turn to movie theaters, which are well attended. Bangkok has several radio and television stations, too. Local markets—selling everything from food to religious articles—are social centers long after the blazing sun goes down.

Bangkok

Made the capital of Thailand in 1782, Bangkok is one of the world's most famous cities. Its thick, hot air is stifling, and the city's canals are foul. But both travelers and residents love it. One of the reasons is its great variety.

An intersection choked with smoky traffic is just yards away from a golden temple casting dark shadows on a lush green garden. Tiny houses on stilts stand next to the stinking canals just down the street from glittering new downtown skyscrapers. For every screaming vendor, there's a Thai with a shy, silent smile. Tourists may find what they want in the expensive shops lining the city streets, but residents of Bangkok will turn to their familiar neighborhood market.

One major piece of architecture, much loved by tourists and Thais alike, is the Grand Palace. It is a walled city founded by King Rama I in 1782 and enlarged in following reigns. In a tree-lined area outside the Palace are ministries, universities, the national museum, national theater, and national art gallery. Here too is the magnificent, gold-roofed Wat Phra Keo, the Temple of the Emerald Buddha. It is the finest Buddhist temple in Thailand.

Much of Bangkok's growth into a major, modern city took place after World War II. No one is quite sure exactly how many people live in Bangkok and the surrounding area. The best guess is that it is six to seven million. All of these people make this sticky tropical city the exciting place it is—whether to live in or to visit.

Thais in North America

A few hundred Thais attend college in the United States and Canada each year. Not many students have learned English in Thailand before coming here, so they must first learn the language before coming to study.

No one can be sure how many true Thais enter North America annually. That is because some recent refugees from camps in Thailand list their nationality as Thai. Actually, these people are more likely to be from Laos or Kampuchea. Nevertheless, both they and true native Thais are coming to live in new lands.

And in many larger cities, Thai restaurants are cropping up, making Thai food popular in North America. Many Thais who start restaurants show their strong ties to their homeland by hanging a picture of the king or the royal family on the restaurant wall. People here try the often hot and spicy Thai food, and through these restaurants many become aware of and interested in the Thai people and their culture.

A Glossary of Useful Thai Terms

ka ru na (gah-ROO-nah) . . . . please
kob kun (kawb-KOON) . . . . thank you
kru (krew) . . . . teacher
lon lean (long LEE-un) . . . . school
mae (MAY-eh) . . . . mother
peong (PER-un) . . . . friend
poo (paw) . . . . father
pu (boo) . . . . grandfather
mai peng ri (MY pen lie) . . . . you're welcome
nam (nahm) . . . . water
sawatdee (SAH-wah-DEE) . . . . hello
wat (waht) . . . . Buddhist temple
ya (yah) . . . . grandmother

More Books about Thailand

Anna and the King of Siam. Landon (Harper and Row)
A Child's Walk through Asia. Levine and Lichter (University of Michigan)
A Family in Thailand. Jacobsen and Kristensen (Franklin Watts)
Fighters, Refugees, Immigrants: A Story of the Hmong. Goldfarb
     (Carolrhoda Books)
The Story of Buddha. Landaw (Auromere)
Take a Trip to Thailand. Lye (Franklin Watts)
A Way of the Buddha. Burland (Dufour)

Things to Do—Research Projects

A group of tribal people called the Hmong were important allies to US troops during the Vietnam War. Many of these people formerly lived by slash-and-burn cultivating. This is a form of agriculture whereby farmers burn forests in order to plant their crops. These primitive Hmong farmers have had to flee to Thailand and are now entering the United States. It has not been as easy for them to adjust to life in the West as it has been for other Asian groups. Try to learn more about what has happened to the Hmong. As you read about their experiences and other current events, keep in mind that it is important to have accurate facts. If the research projects that follow need up-to-date information, look up *Thailand* and *Hmong* in the two publications listed below. They will direct you to articles in your library.

Readers' Guide to Periodical Literature
Children's Magazine Guide

1. Buddhism is one of the largest religions in the world, yet it has no god or gods in the sense that other religions have. Read more about the teachings

of Buddha and the monasteries where Asian men have gathered for centuries to study those teachings.

2. Much has been written about Bangkok, that huge city rich with ancient traditions and the bustle of modern life. About 10% of all Thais have chosen to live in Bangkok, and outsiders flock there each year to explore its sights. Learn more about the attractions of this city for Thais and tourists alike.

More Things to do—Activities

These activities will encourage you to think more about Thailand. They offer interesting group and individual projects you can do at home or at school.

1. Thailand is a country of mountains. In these mountains are many tribal peoples. Check your local library for a map of Thailand and for books such as encyclopedias that describe the lives of these tribes. Try to figure out where the tribes live, what countries they enter when moving about, and what family life is like in these tribes.

2. Rice is the basic food of Thailand. Check your library for books that describe the methods farmers use for planting rice. Learn the difference between hill farming and paddy farming. Besides growing rice as a food, people can use it for other purposes. What products can be made from rice?

3. Jade is one of Thailand's most precious stones. Consult encyclopedias in your library to learn how miners extract jade from the earth. How do artisans work this stone into delicate objects such as jewelry?

4. For a pen pal from Thailand, write to these people:

International Pen Friends
P. O. Box 290065
Brooklyn, NY 11229-0001

Worldwide Pen Friends
P.O. Box 6896
Thousand Oaks, CA 91359

Be sure to tell them what country you want your pen pal to be from. Also, include your age, full name, and address.

Maana and Pani wish you well.

Index